CINCINNATI
BENGALS

BY TOM GLAVE

Published by The Child's World®
1980 Lookout Drive • Mankato, MN 56003-1705
800-599-READ • www.childsworld.com

Acknowledgments
The Child's World®: Mary Berendes, Publishing Director
Red Line Editorial: Editorial direction
The Design Lab: Design
Amnet: Production

Design Element: Dean Bertoncelj/Shutterstock Images
Photographs ©: Darron Cummings/AP Images, cover;
NFL Photos/AP Images, 5, 7, 23; Harvey Eugene Smith/
AP Images, 9; John Sommers/Icon Sportswire, 11; Derek
Jensen, 13; Jay LaPrete/AP Images, 14–15; AP Images, 17;
David Kohl/AP Images, 19; G. Newman Lowrance/
AP Images, 21; Zach Bolinger/Icon Sportswire, 25; MSA/
Icon Sportswire, 27; Athlon Archive/AP Images, 29

ISBN 9781631439926
LCCN 2014959697

Printed in the United States of America
Mankato, MN
July, 2015
PA02265

ABOUT THE AUTHOR

Tom Glave grew up watching football on TV and playing it in the field next to his house. He learned to write about sports at the University of Missouri-Columbia and has written for newspapers in New Jersey, Missouri, Arkansas, and Texas. He lives near Houston, Texas, and cannot wait to play backyard football with his kids Tommy, Lucas, and Allison.

TABLE OF CONTENTS

GO, BENGALS!

Cincinnati Bengals fans got two treats in 1981. First, the team changed its uniform. Black and orange tiger stripes were added. Fans loved the new look. The uniforms are still well known today. But the second treat was even better. The Bengals went to the **Super Bowl** after that season. Cincinnati is still looking for its first championship, however. Let's meet the Bengals.

Cincinnati fans were treated to exciting new uniforms and a strong season from the Bengals in 1981.

WHO ARE THE BENGALS?

The Cincinnati Bengals play in the National Football **League** (NFL). They are one of the 32 teams in the NFL. The NFL includes the American Football Conference (AFC) and the National Football Conference (NFC). The winner of the AFC plays the winner of the NFC in the Super Bowl. The Bengals play in the North Division of the AFC. They have played in two Super Bowls. Cincinnati lost both to the San Francisco 49ers.

Quarterback Boomer Esiason made the Pro Bowl four times in his ten seasons with the Bengals.

WHERE THEY CAME FROM

Coach Paul Brown missed football. He had been fired from the Cleveland Browns in 1963. Brown had helped start that team. He thought Cincinnati needed its own squad. There had been a football team there in the 1930s. It was called the Bengals. So Brown used the same name. The Bengals started in the American Football League (AFL). The league merged with the NFL after the 1969 season. Cincinnati made the **playoffs** in 1970. It was the Bengals' first NFL season.

Paul Brown coached Cincinnati for its first eight years.

WHO THEY PLAY

The Cincinnati Bengals play 16 games each season. With so few games, each one is important. Every year, the Bengals play two games against each of the other three teams in their division. Those teams are the Baltimore Ravens, Pittsburgh Steelers, and Cleveland Browns. The Bengals also play six other teams from the AFC and four from the NFC. The rivalry with the Browns is full of history. Paul Brown helped start both teams. Cincinnati has also had many tough battles with Pittsburgh.

Defensive tackle Geno Atkins (97) tackles Cleveland Browns running back Terrance West in a game on November 6, 2014.

WHERE THEY PLAY

The Bengals joined the NFL in 1970. They started playing in Riverfront Stadium that year. The Bengals shared it with the Cincinnati Reds baseball team. The Bengals played there until 1999. Then Paul Brown Stadium opened in 2000. It is nicknamed "The Jungle." Paul Brown Stadium has 65,515 seats. The Bengals sold out 57 straight home games from 2003 to 2010. The stadium also hosts concerts and college football games. It even hosts a chess tournament every year.

Paul Brown Stadium, also known as "The Jungle," sits about one block away from the Ohio River.

THE FOOTBALL FIELD

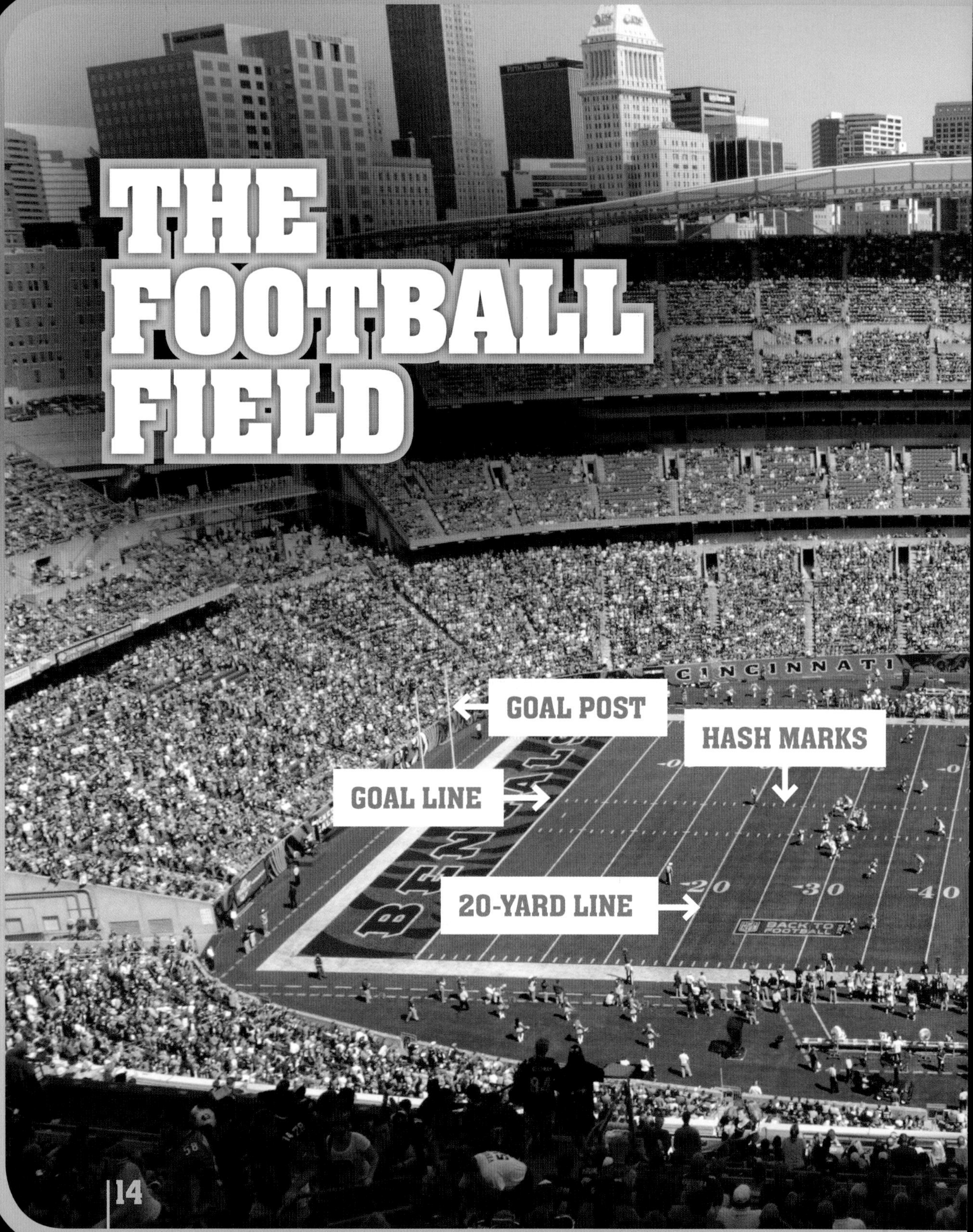
GOAL POST
HASH MARKS
GOAL LINE
20-YARD LINE
CINCINNATI
BENGALS

BENCH AREA

END ZONE

MIDFIELD

END LINE

SIDELINE

BIG DAYS

The Bengals have had some great moments in their history. Here are three of the greatest:

1970—Bengals coach Paul Brown had helped start the Cleveland Browns. But he was fired from the team in 1963. It was important to Brown to beat his old team. It happened for the first time on November 15. It was part of a seven-game winning streak. Cincinnati went on to win the AFC Central.

1975—The Bengals played on *Monday Night Football* on November 17. They beat the Buffalo Bills 33-24. It was Cincinnati's first Monday night win. Quarterback Ken Anderson threw for 447 yards. He led the NFL in passing in 1974 and 1975.

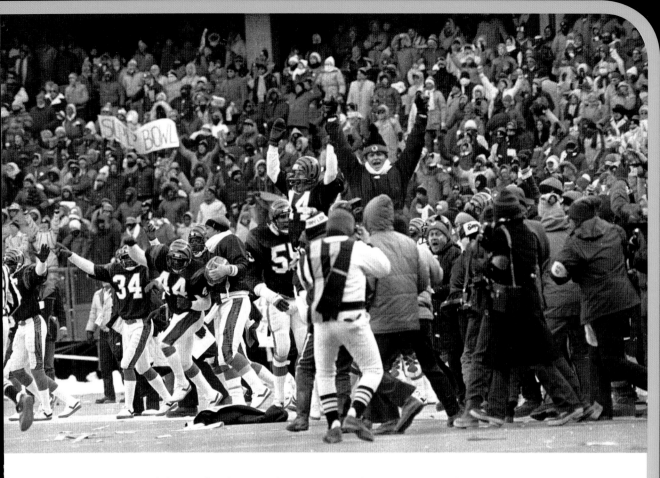

The Bengals celebrate after beating the San Diego Chargers 27–7 in "The Freezer Bowl" on January 10, 1982.

1982—The 1981 Bengals beat Buffalo 28–21 on January 3. It was the first playoff win for the franchise. Then Cincinnati beat the San Diego Chargers in "The Freezer Bowl." The temperature was minus-9°F (minus-23°C) during the game. That win put the Bengals in their first Super Bowl.

TOUGH DAYS

Football is a hard game. Even the best teams have rough games and seasons. Here are some of the toughest times in Bengals history:

1993—Quarterback Boomer Esiason was a fan favorite. He had won the NFL **Most Valuable Player (MVP)** Award in 1988. But he was traded before the 1993 season. The Bengals then lost their first ten games. They finished 3-13. Cincinnati did not win a road game.

2002—The Bengals went 2-14. That is the team's worst season through 2014. Cincinnati allowed almost 29 points per game. That ranked last in the NFL.

2006—The Bengals played the Pittsburgh Steelers on January 8. It was a playoff game. Quarterback Carson

Carson Palmer lies on the field after a hit from Pittsburgh Steelers defensive end Kimo von Oelhoffen in the teams' playoff game on January 8, 2006.

Palmer was hit low on the Bengals' first passing play. He injured his knee badly. Palmer was never the same with Cincinnati. He left the team after the 2010 season.

MEET THE FANS

Bengals fans love wearing black and orange. They wear clothes with tiger stripes to games. The fans also have a special chant. They say "Who dey, who dey, who dey think gonna beat dem Bengals? Nobody!" The chant became popular during the 1981 season. Who Dey is also the team mascot's name. He is a Bengal tiger. Who Dey wears a No. 1 Bengals jersey. He was one of the first NFL mascots.

"Who Dey" is a rallying cry that has united Bengals fans for decades.

HEROES THEN

Left tackle Anthony Munoz was big and athletic. He played in both Cincinnati Super Bowls. Munoz made the **Pro Bowl** every year from 1981 to 1991. He even caught four touchdown passes in his career. Quarterback Ken Anderson was the 1981 NFL MVP. He led the league in passing yards twice. Quarterback Boomer Esiason was the 1988 NFL MVP. Isaac Curtis was very quick. He was one of football's first game-changing receivers. Receiver Cris Collinsworth was a **rookie** in 1981. He had Cincinnati's first 1,000-yard receiving season that year.

Offensive lineman Anthony Munoz's size and agility made him one of the best offensive linemen in NFL history.

HEROES NOW

Wide receiver A. J. Green is tough to stop. He led Cincinnati in catches and receiving yards in 2011. In 2013, he became the first Bengal to record five straight 100-yard games. Quarterback Andy Dalton joined Cincinnati in 2011. He led four fourth-quarter comebacks as a rookie. Defensive tackle Geno Atkins had 12.5 sacks in 2012. Running back Jeremy Hill entered the league in 2014. He had a great first season. Hill scored nine rushing touchdowns. That was third in the NFL.

Running back Jeremy Hill runs with the ball during a playoff game against the Indianapolis Colts on January 4, 2015.

GEARING UP

NFL players wear team uniforms. They wear helmets and pads to keep them safe. Cleats help them make quick moves and run fast. Some players wear extra gear for protection.

THE FOOTBALL

NFL footballs are made of leather. Under the leather is a lining that fills with air to give the ball its shape. The leather has bumps or "pebbles." These help players grip the ball. Laces help players control their throws. Footballs are also called "pigskins" because some of the first balls were made from pig bladders. Today they are made of leather from cows.

Wide receiver A. J. Green made the Pro Bowl in each of his first four NFL seasons.

HELMET

CHIN STRAP

SHOULDER PADS

GLOVES

THIGH PADS

FOOTBALL

SPORTS STATS

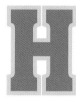 ere are some of the all-time career records for the Cincinnati Bengals. All the stats are through the 2014 season.

RUSHING YARDS

Corey Dillon 8,061

James Brooks 6,447

RECEPTIONS

Chad Johnson 751

Carl Pickens 530

TOTAL TOUCHDOWNS

Pete Johnson 70

Chad Johnson 66

INTERCEPTIONS

Ken Riley 65

Louis Breeden 33

SACKS

Eddie Edwards 47.5

Justin Smith 43.5

POINTS

Jim Breech 1,151

Shayne Graham 779

Quarterback Ken Anderson played his entire 16-year career with the Bengals.

PASSING YARDS

Ken Anderson 32,838

Boomer Esiason 27,149

GLOSSARY

franchise a team that is part of a professional sports league

league an organization of sports teams that compete against each other

Most Valuable Player (MVP) a yearly award given to the top player in the NFL

playoffs a series of games after the regular season that decides which two teams play in the Super Bowl

Pro Bowl the NFL's All-Star game, in which the best players in the league compete

rivalry an ongoing competition between teams that play each other often, over a long time

rookie a player playing in his first season

Super Bowl the championship game of the NFL, played between the winners of the AFC and the NFC

FIND OUT MORE

IN THE LIBRARY

Gigliotti, Jim. *Super Bowl Super Teams*.
New York: Scholastic, 2010.

Gilbert, Sara. *The Story of the Cincinnati Bengals*.
Mankato, MN: Creative Education, 2014.

Stewart, Mark. *The Cincinnati Bengals*.
Chicago: Norwood House, 2013.

ON THE WEB

Visit our Web site for links about the Cincinnati Bengals:
childsworld.com/links

*Note to Parents, Teachers, and Librarians: We routinely verify our Web links to make
sure they are safe and active sites. So encourage your readers to check them out!*

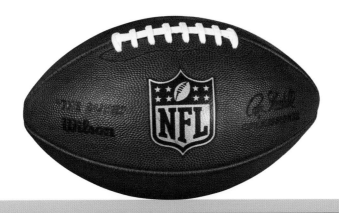

INDEX